(A New Musical)

Book by
Doug Haverty

Music & Lyrics by
Bruce Kimmel

STAGE RIGHTS

www.stagerights.com

A CAROL CHRISTMAS
Copyright © 2018 by Doug Haverty and Bruce Kimmel
All Rights Reserved

All performances and public readings of A CAROL CHRISTMAS are subject to royalties. It is fully protected under the copyright laws of the United States of America, of all countries covered by the International Copyright Union, of all countries covered by the Pan-American Copyright Convention and the Universal Copyright Convention, and all countries with which the United States has reciprocal copyright relations. All rights are strictly reserved.

No part of this book may be reproduced, stored in a retrieval system, or transmitted in any form, by any means, including mechanical, electronic, photocopying, recording, or otherwise, without the prior written permission of the author. Publication of this play does not necessarily imply that it is available for performance by amateurs or professionals. It is strongly recommended all interested parties apply to Steele Spring Stage Rights for performance rights before starting rehearsals or advertising.

No changes shall be made in the play for the purpose of your production without prior written consent. All billing stipulations in your license agreement must be strictly adhered to. No person, firm or entity may receive credit larger or more prominent than that accorded the Author.

For all stage performance inquiries, please contact:

STAGE RIGHTS
www.stagerights.com

A Carol Christmas
(A New Musical)

CAST OF CHARACTERS

WAYNE PEARLMAN, ESQ: An attorney.

WADE PETTIT, ESQ: An attorney.

BLYTHE CURRY: An executive assistant.

FIONA FERRIS: A social media manager.

CAROL FERRIS: An entrepreneur.

AVALON JENKINS: A college intern.

BLAKE WILDING: A medical research doctor.

LEE: Video person.

CODY: Sound person.

LEON WASHINGTON: A medical practitioner.

TRINA CURRY: A young student.

FELIX CURRY: A writer and stay-at-home dad.

JOELLE NEWELL: A deceased businesswoman.

ODETTE WATKINS: A regressional therapist.

MRS. HELEN FORRESTER: A marketer.

MR. HANK FORRESTER: A marketer.

KARINA MARKEYEVICH: An herbalistic healer.

PATTY KEEN: Legal secretary.

JOSIE MILLER: A florist.

HOWIE ROSEN: A stock-broker

MABEL NEVILLE: A Tarot Card reader.

THE HIGH PRIESTESS: Tarot-card-come-to-life female Pope.

DEATH: Tarot Card come-to-life-song-and-dance-man.

Ensemble
- **Children's Choir**
- **Accountants**
- **Designers**
- **The Lovers:** Tarot-card-come-to-life dancers.
- **Office Staffers**

A Carol Christmas
(A New Musical)

TIME & PLACE

The time is the present.

The action takes place mainly at the Pittsburgh, PA headquarters of Lora Co (Carol's Office and Waiting area) And Carol's Loft, Blythe & Felix's Apartment, Forrester & Forrester Conference Room

RUN TIME

90 minutes, no intermission

A Carol Christmas
(A New Musical)

MUSICAL NUMBERS

#1.	Christmas Time Is Here Again / Just Another Christmas	Staff & Carolers
#2.	All I Want for Christmas	Carol
#3.	Spelling Backwards	Trina
#4.	The Message	Joelle
#5.	Close Your Eyes – Parts 1 & 2	Odette
#6.	This Party's Just for You	Forresters & Company
#7.	Meet Cute	Blake & Carol
#7B.	Close Your Eyes – Part 3	Odette
#8.	Separate Ways	Blake
#8A.	All I Want for Christmas (Reprise)	Carol & Kid Chorus
#9.	Owaska Tea – Part 1	Karina
#10.	This Christmas	Fiona
#11.	Little Miracles	Blythe & Trina
#12.	Tarot Cards	Mabel
#13.	I Know Everything, I See Everything	The High Priestess
#14.	The Lovers	Lovers Quartet
#15.	Shuffle Off this Mortal Coil	Death and the Death-Mates
#16.	Nightmare	Company
#16A.	Transition #2	Kid Chorus
#16B.	Transition #3	Kid Chorus
#17.	What Have I Learned	Carol
#18.	Finale / Just Another Christmas	Company
#18A.	After Bows	Company

SCENE 1

At rise, we hear an opening musical prelude. We see a hustle and bustle of employees and clients at the offices of Lora Co waiting to see Carol. We see BLYTHE training AVALON at the reception desk, who is taking fastidious notes on a notepad. FIONA is trying to get their attention. PETIT and PEARLMAN are seated in the waiting Area and two designers, are arguing over the design of a garment. We see accountants, designers and staffers all waiting.

PEARLMAN: Is Carol going to be much longer?

PETTIT: We can't wait.

BLYTHE: She's on a video conference call.

FIONA: Should I come back?

BLYTHE *(to Fiona)*: It's up to you.

(Then, to Avalon)

This is Carol's Calendar. It's like The Bible.

The CHILDREN'S CHOIR enters dressed in Dickensian garb and sings.

SONG #1: CHRISTMAS TIME IS HERE AGAIN / JUST ANOTHER CHRISTMAS

(Singing)
CHRISTMAS TIME IS HERE AGAIN
OUR FAVORITE TIME OF YEAR
CHRISTMAS TREES AGLOW WITH LIGHTS
A TIME FOR CHRISTMAS CHEER

CHRISTMAS STOCKINGS, MISTLETOE
AND FAMILY AND FRIENDS
CHILDREN WAIT FOR SANTA CLAUS
OPENING PRESENTS ON CHRISTMAS DAY
HOPING IT NEVER ENDS

Music changes to a driving vamp. CAROL enters from her office and yells over the music.

CAROL: How charming! You're adorable. Go sing on the fourth floor, they'll love it.

CHILDREN'S CHOIR exits.

Come on, folks! I know it's the day before Christmas, but deadlines are deadlines, let's do this!

She scours the waiting area and chooses two nerdy accountants.

CAROL (CONT'D): Accountants, in my office! In five!

She exits into her office followed by two STAFFERS.

ALL:
JUST ANOTHER CHRISTMAS
SHOULD BE TIME FOR CELEBRATING AND FUN
BUT THERE WON'T BE FUN TILL OUR WORK IS DONE
WE'LL BE ON THE RUN
WE'LL BE LUCKY TO LEAVE

JUST ANOTHER CHRISTMAS
JUST A TIME FOR DEADLINES WE'VE GOT TO MEET
WE'LL BE ON OUR FEET, TILL THE WORK'S COMPLETE
WE'RE ALREADY BEAT
JUST FORGET CHRISTMAS EVE

THOUGH FRIENDS AND FAMILY AWAIT
WE'RE CLEARLY GONNA BE LATE
I'VE STILL GOT PRESENTS TO BUY
BUT WE'RE JUST
STUCK HERE, WILL WE EVER GET HOME
IS THERE AN END TO THIS DAY
WE CAN PRAY
BUT THEN THERE'S ALWAYS ONE MORE MEETING
THERE'S ALWAYS ONE MORE DEADLINE
THERE'S ALWAYS ONE MORE PROJECT
AND SO WE'VE GOT TO STAY

Music continues underneath.

FIONA *(to Avalon)*: Hi, I'm Fiona, Carol's niece. Who are you?

AVALON *(to Fiona)*: Hi, I'm the new intern.

FIONA: And she hasn't eaten you alive yet?

Looks at her watch.

Well, it's early.

She exits.

BLAKE *(to Avalon as he approaches with flowers)*: Could you tell her Blake is here?

BLYTHE: Hi, Blake.

BLAKE: What are the chances of squeezing me in?

BLYTHE: Impossible.

BLAKE: That good, huh? I thought, maybe Christmas Eve; things might slow down a tad.

BLYTHE: Not a tadette.

AVALON *(to Blake, indicating the flowers)*: Would you like some water for those?

BLAKE *(to Avalon)*: Who are you?

AVALON *(to Blake)*: The new intern.

BLAKE: And she hasn't eaten you alive yet?

BLYTHE *(to Blake)*: Sit. I'll see what we can do.

> *She reads a text on her phone.*

(Upset)

Oh, God.

AVALON *(notices Blythe is upset)*: Is anything wrong?

BLYTHE *(reading her phone/text)*: My husband's had to call the nurse again. Our daughter, Trina, has a heart problem.

AVALON: I'm sorry. Is it serious?

BLYTHE: Some days are better than others.

AVALON: Go. I'll keep the peasants from storming the gates.

BLYTHE: But there's too much to do. Thank God my husband is with her.

> *Music changes as lights Isolate BLYTHE.*

(Singing)
JUST ANOTHER CHRISTMAS
AND MY DAUGHTER NEEDS ME BUT I'M STILL HERE
AND I WILL BE HERE HOURS MORE I FEAR
THAT'S ALREADY CLEAR, SHOULD I STAY, SHOULD I GO

> *Music tempo changes and lights Isolate AVALON.*

AVALON:
JUST ANOTHER CHRISTMAS
WILL I SINK OR SWIM IN THIS CRAZY PLACE
EVERYTHING'S A RACE, ONE GIGANTIC CHASE
PEOPLE IN YOUR FACE, I'LL JUST GO WITH THE FLOW

> *Lights isolate BLAKE.*

BLAKE:
    I DON'T KNOW WHY I CAME BY
    IT'S ALWAYS PIE IN THE SKY
    SHE'S JUST TOO BUSY TO CARE
    BUT STILL I
    SHOW UP AND I SIT HERE AND WAIT
    IT'S LIKE DETENTION IN SCHOOL
    WHAT A FOOL

    Lights Isolate BLAKE, BLYTHE, and AVALON.

AVALON, BLAKE & FIONA:
    BECAUSE THERE'S ALWAYS ONE MORE MEETING
    THERE'S ALWAYS ONE MORE DEADLINE
    THERE'S ALWAYS ONE MORE PROJECT
    THAT YOU CAN'T OVERRULE

    Music continues underneath. CAROL enters from her office with two exiting ACCOUNTANTS.

CAROL *(snapping)*: Give me projections that actually make sense in dollars and cents.

    (To Blythe)

Who are all these people?

BLYTHE: You called them.

CAROL: You! Designers! Bring those fabric swatches and they'd better not be ugly. In here! In five!

    CAROL exits into her office with two designers. EVERYONE sings and they are joined by the GIRLS CHORUS in counterpoint.

ALL:
    JUST ANOTHER CHRISTMAS
    JUST ANOTHER HOLIDAY WE DON'T SHARE
    AND SHE DOESN'T CARE AND IT ISN'T FAIR
    BUT WE GRIN AND BEAR IT, THERE'S NOTHING TO DO

    JUST ANOTHER CHRISTMAS
    YES, A TIME FOR CELEBRATING AND FUN
    TELL ME WHERE'S THE FUN, WHEN THE WORK'S NOT DONE
    WHEN WE'RE ON THE RUN, AND WE JUST WANT TO LEAVE
    JUST ANOTHER CHRISTMAS (AND WE JUST WANT TO LEAVE)
    JUST ANOTHER CHRISTMAS (AND WE JUST WANT TO LEAVE)
    JUST ANOTHER CHRISTMAS (AND WE SO WANT TO LEAVE)
    SO WE GET HOME IN TIME FOR CHRISTMAS EVE.

ALL (CONT'D):
JUST ANOTHER CHRISTMAS!

> *On Musical Playoff, we shift to Carol's Office. As we shift:*

BLYTHE *(to Avalon)*: Grab those agreements and follow me.

BLAKE: Uh... I'll just go "laptop" over here in the corner.

> *AVALON and BLYTHE cross in to Carol's office. Lights isolate Carol's office.*

CAROL *(to Blythe)*: Who is this person?

BLYTHE: This is Avalon. Remember I told you. She's our Winter-Intern.

AVALON: Hi, Carol. I love your brand: "Clothes for girls who eat." It's just—

CAROL *(to Avalon)*: You're not afraid to work on Christmas Eve or Christmas Day or any of those horrible days between the holidays?

AVALON: No. In fact, I—

CAROL: And you're getting college credit for this and you're not expecting to get paid?

AVALON: Right.

CAROL *(to Blythe)*: Can we clone her?

BLYTHE: I'll put that on the "to do" list.

CAROL: Did we hear from Wilhelm?

BLYTHE: Holiday. Cancun.

CAROL: Yamamoto?

BLYTHE: Vacation: Fiji.

CAROL: Gregorio?

BLYTHE: Skiing. Alps.

CAROL: Ooooh, I hate that. Everyone's off doing something frivolous just because it's "Christmas." I feel like I'm running a race with molasses on my shoes.

> *FIONA enters with a report and puts it on Carol's desk.*

(To Fiona)

Why didn't you interoffice that? Why aren't you in your office?

FIONA: You wanted this Social Media Marketing Campaign right away and I wanted to re-invite you to my annual party tonight.

CAROL: Okay. Missions accomplished.

FIONA: It's a Christmakuh occasion because I'm dating a Jewish stock-broker.

CAROL *(to Fiona)*: Good for you. I'm sure you still have work to do.

FIONA: Yes, of course. I notice the sentry station outside is unoccupied, do you want me to hold down the fort?

CAROL: I want you to go put in a full day's work. I say this with all the love an aunt can muster: out!

> *FIONA exits.*
>
> *(Then to Avalon)*

Why are you writing like that?

AVALON: I'm learning.

CAROL: Go.

> *BLYTHE and AVALON exit as BLAKE pokes his head in.*
>
> *(To Blake)*

What are you doing here? Did I butt-dial you?

BLAKE: I had kind of a holiday proposal.

> *He hands her flowers.*

CAROL: I have told you a thousand times, I will not marry you.

BLAKE: This is not a "till death do us part" thing. It's shorter.

CAROL: I am severely swamped. If you want to wait out there, I cannot make any promises that I will get to you before the new year.

BLAKE: I'll pop up my tent.

> *He exits.*
>
> *BLYTHE and AVALON usher LEE and CODY in with video equipment and they set it up.*

BLYTHE *(to Carol)*: Lee and Cody are here to shoot your promo. And we've got Pearlman and Pettit out there. They've been waiting—

CAROL: Attorneys here on Christmas Eve? Great. Send them in after we finish here.

AVALON: They don't invoice you for waiting, do they?

CAROL *(to Blythe)*: Give them a Christmas cookie and tell them you hope they enjoyed our Office Christmas party. That way it will be a non-billable visit.

> *AVALON and BLYTHE exit to waiting area.*

Do you have the copy? Quick! Let me see it.

CODY: Here you go.

> *Hands her a sheet with large text on it.*

CAROL *(reading)*: It's horrible! Who wrote this?

LEE *(as they are setting up)*: You did.

CAROL: Oh. Well, I guess it's not so bad. I'll perk it up a little.

CODY: Of course.

CAROL: Ready?

LEE: And five, four...

> *Then he switches to fingers for silence, three, two, one.*

CAROL *(Carol suddenly becomes her sweet TV personality)*: Hi, ya'll. It's Carol here. Honeys, have I got a special for you. We got some darlin' new outfits here at FOR GIRLS WHO EAT. And, believe me when I tell you I know that your little wallets are just plum tuckered out, so my accounting department has devised the most spectacular Flex-Pay you're ever gonna see you in your entire life. So, watch here for our New Year's show, same time, same channel. And don't you feel no pressure to go on no diet for New Year's. Huh-uh. Carol'll take care of ya. You know I will!

> *She smiles.*

(Beat)

Cut!

(To Lee and Cody)

Get that down to editing. Now. Out.

> *PEARLMAN & PETTIT enter.*

All right. What do you clowns want and make it snappy. I don't want to have to castrate anyone this early.

PEARLMAN: It's about your late partner's estate.

CAROL: Joelle? I thought it was all handled.

PETTIT: There is one more detail.

PEARLMAN: A video that is to be given to you on the first Christmas Eve following her death.

CAROL: That crazy woman is now haranguing me from her grave?

PEARLMAN: If you'll sign here we can turn over the DVD.

CAROL *(as she signs the document)*: There. Happy?

> *BLYTHE and AVALON enter.*

What now?

BLYTHE: I'm sorry, Carol. It's about the bonus checks.

CAROL: Let's torch them and see if anyone notices.

BLYTHE: They just came up from Payroll. Did you want to sign them now?

CAROL: No. Not ever.

BLYTHE: But I thought you wanted—

CAROL: I never wanted to sign each one. That was _your_ idea. Do you think anyone will notice that I actually John Hancocked their bonus checks? I think not.

BLYTHE: Some might.

CAROL: It's not even a reward anymore. It's expected.

BLYTHE: I'll rubber-stamp them then. Did you want to hand them out?

CAROL: I don't know everyone's name. You do it.

BLYTHE: I think it will mean more coming from you.

CAROL: They COME from me.

AVALON: I just have to say that we watch your show all the time at the dorm.

CAROL: You do? Isn't that fascinating? How often have you ordered anything?

AVALON: Well, I want to when—

CAROL: There is a huge difference between those who want want want and those that do do do.

AVALON: Once I'm out in the world and working—

CAROL: Did your parents give you a credit card?

AVALON: It's for emergencies only.

CAROL *(to Avalon)*: I rest my case.

(To Pearlman and Pettit)

You're still here? This DVD isn't going to blow up, is it?

PEARLMAN: Well, as you know, we represent several admirable charities.

PETTIT: And since it's year end, you may want to—

CAROL: I've got all the write-offs I need. I have no sympathy for people who won't work.

PEARLMAN: We understand.

CAROL: Good. Goodbye.

PETTIT: Merry Christmas.

CAROL: Yeah, whatever. Out, out. Enjoy the party!

They exit as BLAKE sneaks in.

(Then, to Blake)

You're not letting someone die on an operating table, are you?

BLAKE: No, you know I don't practice anymore. I'm in research now.

CAROL: Great. I give you carte blanche to experiment on any one of my employees.

BLAKE: I'll hang out a little longer.

He exits.

AVALON *(as she hands Carol a stack of messages)*: These are all urgent.

CAROL: Aren't they all?

BLYTHE *(holding up a larger stack)*: No, these are non-urgent.

CAROL: Can't you call them back, Blythe?

BLYTHE: They all want to speak to you personally.

CAROL: They just want to wish me Merry, Happy Anything. I haven't got time!

> *(To Blythe)*

You know what? Hold all my calls. I need a "me" minute.

> *She starts to shoo them out and notices AVALON's dropped jaw.*

Intern-whose-name-I-can't-remember, un-drop your jaw. Yes, I'm not like I am on TV. There I have to be charming and folksy and sunny. Here I have to be cutthroat and flagrant and stormy. I am the turbine that powers this enterprise and some days I have to go to DEFCON 1. Everyone out!

AVALON *(writing it all down)*: Okay. Thank you for explaining that. I really—

CAROL: When I send you out, a response is not required.

> *BLYTHE and AVALON exit. CAROL is alone. She leans against the door, takes a breath and gathers strength. She sings:*

SONG #2: ALL I WANT FOR CHRISTMAS

> *(Singing)*

THEY SAY THAT I AM DRIVEN
WELL, I GUESS THAT THAT'S A GIVEN
THAT'S THE PRICE THAT YOU PAY WHEN YOU LIVE IN
THE WORLD I DO
IF I SEE THE CHRISTMAS SPIRIT
I DON'T WANT TO GO ANYWHERE NEAR IT
CHRISTMAS JOY? DON'T WANT TO HEAR IT
IT'S ALL TRUE
CHRISTMAS COMES BUT ONCE A YEAR
THAT'S FAR TOO OFTEN FOR ME— THAT'S CLEAR

ALL I WANT FOR CHRISTMAS IS FOR CHRISTMAS TO BE DONE
THERE'S NO STOPPING CHRISTMAS ONCE THE DAMN THING HAS BEGUN
GOT NO TIME FOR CHRISTMAS CAROLS OR A CHRISTMAS TREE
YOU CAN JUST KEEP CHRISTMAS FAR FROM ME

ALL I WANT FOR CHRISTMAS IS THE MONEY ROLLING IN
PEOPLE CALLING, PEOPLE BUYING, LET THAT JOY BEGIN
ALL THE REST IS WINDOW DRESSING AND IT'S ALL A BORE
I'D LIKE TO PUT CHRISTMAS ON "IGNORE."

WILL I HAVE MYSELF A MERRY LITTLE CHRISTMAS— NO, I WON'T
DO I HAVE CHESTNUTS ROASTING ON AN OPEN FIRE— NO, I DON'T
WHEN THEY SING ABOUT THOSE REINDEER,

CAROL (CONT'D):
    WELL IT MAKES ME WANT TO SCREAM
    SANTA DOWN MY CHIMNEY IS LIKE HAVING A BAD DREAM

    ALL I WANT FOR CHRISTMAS IS FOR ALL OF THIS TO END
    CHRISTMAS EVERY FOUR YEARS, THAT'S WHAT I WOULD RECOMMEND
    MISTLETOE AND OLD SAINT NICK DON'T INTEREST ME AT ALL
    DID I ONCE LIKE CHRISTMAS? WELL, I REALLY DON'T RECALL
    CHRISTMAS WISHES MAKE ME DIZZY
    I'M TOO BUSY BEING BUSY
    JUST ONE THING I WANT ON CHRISTMAS DAY
    AND THAT'S FOR YULETIDES AND SLEIGH RIDES
    AND JINGLE BELLS AND SANTA CLAUS AND CHRISTMAS
    TO GO AWAY.

        Lights blackout.

SCENE 2

Lights fade up on Blythe & Felix's house. LEON, a medical practitioner/nurse is sitting next to TRINA, who is in a chair. FELIX stands nearby.

LEON: Okay? Breathing better now, Trina?

TRINA: Yes. Can we take off the nose hose?

LEON: Yes, we can!

TRINA: Yay!

LEON removes the oxygen nose tube and wraps it up.

FELIX: I knew she overdid it today. Choir, party, Christmas play—

TRINA: I didn't do all those things, Daddy. I sang with the choir, that's all.

FELIX: But you went to the play. You went to the party.

TRINA: I watched. How much energy does that take?

FELIX: Evidently a lot.

Felix's phone rings.

(Into phone)

Hi, Blythe.

An isolated spotlight fades up on BLYTHE on her cellphone.

BLYTHE *(into phone)*: How is she?

FELIX: Better. Trina, re-assure your mother.

TRINA *(into phone)*: Daddy said you need to hear my cheerful voice.

BLYTHE *(into phone)*: You gave us quite a scare.

TRINA *(into phone)*: Medical Practitioner Leon is here and he made me breathe better.

BLYTHE *(into phone)*: I'm so glad Medical Practitioner Leon is there.

TRINA *(into phone)*: Yeah. It was just that scary-feels-like-you're-drowning-but-you're-not-in-water thing. But not as bad as before.

BLYTHE *(into phone)*: Trina, I know it's an exciting day, but you have to pace—

TRINA *(into phone)*: Mom, are you coming home soon? We have to make the Candy Cane cookies for Santa.

BLYTHE *(into phone)*: Yes, I'm trying to leave now.

TRINA *(into phone)*: The dough is chillin' in the fridge.

BLYTHE *(into phone)*: Perfect.

She hangs up.

Light fades on BLYTHE.

TRINA *(to Felix)*: Mission accomplished.

> *Hangs up phone.*

TRINA (CONT'D): She's re-assured now.

> *She hands the phone back to Felix.*

LEON: So, how do you get through a day and not over-exert yourself?

TRINA: I let my mind do all the jumping around. I do puzzles and brain games. I write stories.

LEON: Really?

TRINA: One of my favorite things is to wrestle with words.

LEON: What do you mean?

TRINA: I have this special word-working game I play.

LEON: What is it?

TRINA: I spell backwards.

LEON: Backwards?

TRINA: I take a word and spell it backwards and sometimes you get a new word.

LEON: Aha. Clever.

TRINA: The hardest words are names. 'Cause when you make them go backwards, it usually sounds like a burp.

> *(Discovering)*

But not yours! "Leon" backwards is "Noel." How perfect is that for today?

LEON: I never realized that. That is so cool

> *Music starts.*

TRINA: I've always done it ever since I could spell.

SONG #3: SPELLING BACKWARDS

> *(Singing)*

I CAN'T TELL YOU WHY I DO IT
I CAN'T TELL YOU WHY AT ALL
I KNOW IT'S ABSURD
BUT WHEN I SEE A WORD
THEN I AUTOMATICALLY SPELL IT BACKWARDS AND
SOMETIMES THERE'S A NEW WORD THAT'S THERE
SOMETIMES WHEN YOU SEE WORDS SPELLED BACKWARDS
YOU GET A WHOLE NEW WORD TO SHARE.

> *(Speaking)*

Can you find a reward in a drawer? You can, because reward is drawer spelled backwards!

TRINA (CONT'D):
>IF I'M FEELING DOWN AND DREARY
>IF I NEED A PICK-ME-UP
>HERE'S WHAT DOES THE TRICK
>I GET CHEERED UP QUICK
>THAT'S 'CAUSE EVERY TIME I SEE WORDS IN FRONT OF ME
>SUDDENLY THEY JUST REARRANGE
>EVERY TIME I SEE WORDS IN FRONT OF ME
>THEN THOSE WORDS BEGIN TO CHANGE
>>*(Speaks)*

Do you think a dog believes in god? Of course, because dog is god spelled backwards! I can even make up new words— like "oops" is "spoo" spelled backwards. Spoo are people who aren't very nice— spoo people.

>>*(Singing)*
>WHENEVER I'M FEELING DEPRESSED
>WHENEVER I'M STRAINED AND I'M STRESSED
>I JUST EAT DESSERTS— WHY?
>BECAUSE DESSERTS IS STRESSED SPELLED BACKWARDS
>DID YOU KNOW THAT STAR CAN BE RATS
>DID YOU KNOW THAT STAB CAN BE BATS
>DID YOU KNOW THAT PART CAN BE TRAP
>DID YOU KNOW A PAL HAS A LAP
>DID YOU KNOW THAT NUTS CAN JUST STUN
>DID YOU KNOW THAT NOW CAN BE WON
>DID YOU KNOW THAT TIME CAN EMIT
>DID YOU KNOW THAT TIPS CAN BE SPIT
>DID YOU KNOW THAT PAT IS A TAP
>DID YOU KNOW THAT PAN IS A NAP
>DID YOU KNOW THAT DEER CAN BE REED
>DID YOU KNOW THAT DEEP CAN BE PEED
>YES, WHEN YOU LACK WORDS
>SPELL SOME BACKWARDS
>YOU MIGHT JUST FIND SOME NICE SURPRISES THERE
>YOU'LL FIND NEW WORDS, ALL SHAPES AND SIZES THERE
>>*(Speaks)*

Like does a gateman have to wear a nametag— yes, because gateman is nametag spelled backwards!

>>*(Singing)*
>NOW YOU KNOW MY LITTLE SECRET
>NOW YOU KNOW THE GAME I PLAY

TRINA (CONT'D):
YOU CAN PLAY IT, TOO
IT'S A BREEZE IT'S TRUE
ALL THE FUN THAT YOU CAN HAVE SPELLING BACKWARDS
AND ALL THE WORDS THAT COME SHINING THROUGH
EVERY TIME YOU ARE SPELLING BACKWARDS
A WORLD OF WORDS JUST WAITS FOR YOU

  Blackout.

SCENE 3

Later. BLYTHE and AVALON are looking over CAROL's shoulder.

AVALON: It is so weird to be looking at next Summer's catalog in the middle of winter.

CAROL: That's how we have to do it. This is actually late. Get those final corrections down to the art department.

BLYTHE: Okay.

She gathers up the mock ups.

CAROL *(notices Avalon writing notes)*: I want a copy of everything you've written.

AVALON: Sure.

CAROL: Okay. Out! I have to watch this DVD.

BLYTHE and AVALON exit. CAROL puts the DVD into a player. Lights Isolate a flat screen area and we eventually see JOELLE, Carol's former business partner.

JOELLE: Hello, Carol. If you're viewing this, then it means that you outlived me, you bitch.

CAROL: Oh, dear Lord!

JOELLE: Uh-uh-uh. No comments from the peanut gallery. I know you're commenting. Stop! Don't. I want you to listen to me very carefully.

CAROL: I do not have time for this nonsense.

JOELLE: You see, I've set up a little adventure for you, dearheart. I know how much you hate Christmas, but I've got three "year-end" festive surprises for you. I've made three entries on your calendar-of-calendars. You will have three visits this Christmas Eve.

CAROL: I'm not listening.

SONG #4: THE MESSAGE

JOELLE:
YOU NEVER LISTENED TO A SINGLE THING I SAID
NOW THAT I'M DEAD IT'S TIME YOU DO
I'VE ARRANGED A LITTLE SHOW AND TELL
TIME TO LISTEN UP AND HEAR ME WELL
TIME TO SEE THE PERSON YOU'VE BECOME
AND THE TRUTH MIGHT LEAVE YOU FEELING NUMB

CAROL: I have work to do.

JOELLE:
> YOU'RE SO CONSUMED WITH WORK
> YOU LIVE IT NIGHT AND DAY
> YOU CRAVE THE CHAOS YOU CREATE
> YOU'VE FORGOTTEN WHAT IT IS TO GIVE
> NOT TO MENTION WHAT IT IS TO LIVE
> JUST A SOULLESS, TOUGH, WELL-OILED MACHINE

CAROL: Oh, please!

(Singing)
> AND YOU KNOW EXACTLY WHAT I MEAN

JOELLE:
> I WENT TO A LOT OF TROUBLE
> BUT I DID IT FOR A WORTHY CAUSE
> PERHAPS YOU CAN LEARN SOME THINGS,
> SOME THINGS THAT MIGHT JUST GIVE YOU PAUSE
> IF YOU'RE SMART YOU WILL TAKE THE TROUBLE
> TO GET OUT OF YOUR LITTLE BUBBLE
> SEE YOURSELF IN THE PAST AND PRESENT
> WHAT YOU SEE MIGHT NOT BE THAT PLEASANT
> AND THE FUTURE, YOU'RE ABOUT TO LEARN
> TIME TO MEND YOUR WAYS BEFORE YOU CRASH AND BURN

She tries to turn off the DVD with the remote. JOELLE laughs demonically.

CAROL: What the hell?

JOELLE:
> REMOTELY SPEAKING THAT REMOTE WON'T HELP YOU NOW
> I'VE SAID THE THINGS I HAD TO SAY
> IF YOU'RE SMART YOU'LL LISTEN AND YOU'LL FIND
> FIND THE THINGS THAT GIVE YOU PEACE OF MIND
> GOT TO RUN, I'M OFF, IT'S TIME TO FLY
> FIND YOUR LIFE OR LIFE WILL PASS YOU BY

CAROL is successful in shutting off the DVD player and lights fade out on JOELLE. BLYTHE and AVALON enter.

BLYTHE: Sorry to interrupt.

CAROL: Not as sorry as I am for having watched this stupid DVD.

BLYTHE: Your three o' clock is here.

CAROL: What three o' clock?

BLYTHE: Odette.

CAROL: What are you talking about?

BLYTHE: Well, she's been on the calendar for months now. I thought you booked the appointment. I didn't.

CAROL: Oh. Joelle, you old so and so. I guess—

> *She stops.*

Give me a second, then send Odette in.

AVALON: Can I get you anything?

CAROL: Yes. I'd like <u>you</u> to keep everyone working until six PM tonight. Just because there is cake at four doesn't mean the day is over. Can you "get <u>that</u> for me"?

AVALON: I don't know if—

CAROL: Use your noggin.

> *She exits to her powder room.*

AVALON: What magic thing does Odette do?

BLYTHE: She is a Regressional Therapist.

AVALON: What's that?

BLYTHE: Someone who hypnotizes you, shows you what you did and then is also a licensed therapist so they can help you deal with what you've done.

AVALON: I missed that option on career day.

> *She and AVALON exit.*
>
> *CAROL re-enters from the powder room. From offstage we hear BLYTHE.*

BLYTHE *(offstage)*: You can go in now.

ODETTE *(as she enters)*: Hello, Carol!

CAROL: Why are you so chipper?

ODETTE: Just happy to see you... in your element... thriving... busy... racing to the finish line.

CAROL: I didn't book you today, Joelle did.

ODETTE: Still "blaming" things on the dearly departed business partner.

CAROL: I'm not doing that.

ODETTE: I thought we had progressed past the blame game.

CAROL: Don't get all therapist-y on me.

ODETTE: Right. Don't want to do that.

CAROL: Joelle told me on a DVD.

ODETTE: I see.

CAROL: Evidently she spent her last days putting together some juicy life lesson she had to impart to me, initiated on Christmas Eve.

ODETTE: Clever. She knew you'd be frazzled. Shall we get to work?

CAROL: Yes.

ODETTE: Can you do the deep, cleansing breaths on your own, or do you want me to take twice as much time while I count them down?

CAROL *(exhaling big time)*: I'm already on three.

ODETTE: You're such a good student; not at all like the woman I met in Paris having a panic attack in between fashion shows.

CAROL *(inhaling)*: Reminding me of that is not helping me relax.

> *Exhales.*

ODETTE: Can you get there yourself, or do you need me to guide you?

CAROL: Take me away! Take me back!

ODETTE: Good. Free your mind.

> *Music comes in.*

Concentrate on my voice. Float. You're feeling weightless.

SONG #5: CLOSE YOUR EYES

> *(Singing)*
> CLOSE YOUR EYES AND JUST RELAX YOUR MIND
> CLOSE YOUR EYES AND LET'S SEE WHAT WE FIND
> WHEN WE GO BACK
> THINGS THAT WE'LL DISCOVER
> THINGS THAT WE'LL UNCOVER
> BACK TO THE CHRISTMAS PAST OF LONG AGO
> AND MAYBE YOU'LL FIND
> THERE'S SOMETHING NEW YOU DIDN'T KNOW

ODETTE: What do you see, Carol?

CAROL: I can't tell— It's all fuzzy, blurry.

ODETTE: Just concentrate. Bring it into focus.

> *(Singing)*
> CLOSE YOUR EYES AND LET'S GO BACK IN TIME
> CLOSE YOUR EYES, AND LET THE MEM'RIES CLIMB
> UP AND GREET YOU
> TIME TO JUST UNWIND NOW
> TIME TO CLEAR YOUR MIND NOW
> BACK TO THE PERSON THAT YOU USED TO BE
> YOU'RE DRIFTING BACK TO THE PERSON THAT WE WANT TO SEE
> *(Singing)*

Where are we?

CAROL: Christmas Party, where I first worked.

A CAROL CHRISTMAS

ODETTE: Good. What do you see?

CAROL: Forrester & Forrester— husband and wife, they had a marketing company. It's my first office Christmas party. I'm a college intern.

> *The music shifts and the stage transforms to a flashback of the Forrester & Forrester Christmas party.*

FORRESTER: Everybody! We're so glad you're all here. As the year draws to a close and we tally and rally, we realize that our strongest asset is you.

MRS. FORRESTER: Each one of you make an invaluable contribution from our first employee ever, Miss Julia Murphy, to our newest recruit, fresh out of college, Carol Ann Ferris.

> *She pulls in JULIA and then CAROL.*

FORRESTER: It's been a great year. Now, let's celebrate.

SONG #6: *THIS PARTY'S JUST FOR YOU*

MRS. FORRESTER:
HAVE A DRINK
EAT SOME FOOD
AND THEN GRAB SOMEONE AND DANCE
LET'S CELEBRATE THIS YEAR
SUCCESS— LET'S GIVE A CHEER
WE'RE GLAD THAT YOU'RE ALL HERE
THIS PARTY'S JUST FOR YOU
FOR ALL THE THINGS YOU DO

ALL EMPLOYEES: Party!

MR. FORRESTER:
LOOK AROUND
WE'RE A TEAM
IT'S OUR WAY OF SHOWING THANKS
SO, MINGLE, MEET NEW FRIENDS
CATCH UP ON ODDS AND ENDS
AND BLESS OUR DIVIDENDS
YOUR BONUS CHECKS ARE HERE
AND BETTER YET— THEY'LL CLEAR

ALL EMPLOYEES: Party!

(Singing)
IT'S OUR FAVORITE TIME OF THE YEAR THAT'S HOW
WE ALL FEEL 'CAUSE WE'RE HERE TOGETHER
IT'S OUR FAVORITE TIME OF THE YEAR SO
DRINK A TOAST

ALL EMPLOYEES (CONT'D):
TO OUR HOST
FORRESTER AND FORRESTER
THEY'RE THE MOST
WONDERFUL EMPLOYERS EVER

SO WE'LL DRINK
EAT SOME FOOD
AND THEN GRAB SOMEONE AND DANCE
WE'LL CELEBRATE THIS YEAR
SUCCESS— LET'S GIVE A CHEER
WE'RE GLAD THAT WE'RE ALL HERE
THIS PARTY'S JUST BEGUN
SO BRING ON ALL THE FUN
    (Speaking)
Party! Party!

> *EVERYBODY dances. CAROL stands watching and FORRESTER pulls her in she dances with everyone. At the end of the number, the EMPLOYEES scatter. BLAKE and CAROL head over to the punch bowl. There is only one cup left and they both reach for it.*

BLAKE: Oh, sorry. Go ahead.

CAROL: No. You take it. You're probably thirstier.

BLAKE: Odd, that they would run out of cups.

CAROL: There's plenty of punch. I could just tip the bowl and you could slurp.

BLAKE: I don't remember you from last year's party.

CAROL: No, you don't. I'm Carol. I'm an intern.

BLAKE: I'm Blake. I'm a relative.

> *They shake hands. CAROL gets a shock from BLAKE's hand.*

Oh, Sorry. Static electricity.

CAROL: Must be.

BLAKE: Forrester is my uncle. I'm in Med School and they always take me in during the holidays. And as a matter of fact, I've been an intern here before, too.

CAROL: You have?

BLAKE: He'd say to me, "Blake, if that doctor thing doesn't work out, you'll always have a job here."

CAROL: How is the doctor thing working out?

BLAKE: If I ever get there. It's tough—

He stops.

CAROL: Really, take the cup. You're the nephew, I'm just an intern.

BLAKE: We could share.

He sips and refills the cup.

Here— medically speaking— this side of the cup is relatively germ-free. So you're interning at an advertising agency? What do you eventually want to do? What's your dream job?

CAROL: Wow. Pretty heady stuff for standing around the cupless Christmas punch bowl.

BLAKE: It's part of my training as a doctor: cut to the chase, get through as many people as possible each hour.

CAROL: And that philosophy could work in a lot of jobs.

BLAKE: Yes. So?

CAROL: An entrepreneur; have my own brand... a line of clothes.

BLAKE *(as he refills the cup)*: Red carpet couture? Sportswear? Bathing suits? Wedding dresses? I won't hold you to it.

CAROL: Actually something more everyday-that-could-double-as-evening-wear. Practical, fun, distinct and variable.

BLAKE: And you think soaking up strategies from my uncle's advertising firm will help you with this quest?

CAROL: Yes. Marketing a brand is almost as important as the product. Did you know that as many years as they take to develop a perfume, they'll spend twice as long developing the bottle? So, what kind of medicine?

BLAKE: Heart surgery.

CAROL: Not brain surgery?

BLAKE: I want to fix broken hearts.

CAROL: What about broken brains?

(Beat)

It was nice meeting you, "Blake."

BLAKE: Would you like to go sit, share a table?

CAROL: Sure, but just know that nothing's going to come of this. You'll go back to Med School and do all that doctor prep stuff and not have a minute of time for yourself— or anyone else— until you've set up a practice and signed the loan papers in what— seven years?

BLAKE: I see an empty table right over there.

CAROL: Yes. With one chair.

BLAKE: It's our table.

They cross to the table, he finds another chair and they sit.

This is like one of those old movies?

CAROL: What do you mean?

Music in.

BLAKE: Those classic, screwball comedies where two mis-matched people "meet cute."

CAROL: Is that what we're doing?

BLAKE: I don't know, but...

SONG #7: MEET CUTE

(Singing)
I SEE YOU, YOU SEE ME
AFTER THAT IT'S JUST GRAVITY
WILL WE SOAR OR JUST NEED A PARACHUTE
LIKE A MAGNET
I AM DRAWN TO YOU
YOU ARE DRAWN TO ME
WITTY REPARTEE FOLLOWS
AND THERE'S REALLY NOTHING TO DO
YOU JUST ROLL WITH THE PUNCHES WHEN YOU MEET CUTE

CAROL: An old movie, huh. Screwball?

(Singing)
I EYE YOU, YOU EYE ME
IS IT PROSE, IS IT POETRY
WILL WE CLICK, STICK AROUND OR GET THE BOOT
A DILEMMA
STILL YOU MAKE ME LAUGH
STILL I LIKE YOUR STYLE
WHEN YOU FLASH THAT SMILE, OH WELL
I JUST TURN TO MUSH, YEAH IT'S TRUE
THAT'S THE WAY IT ALL CRUMBLES WHEN YOU MEET CUTE

SURE THIS GUY IS A CHARMER
SHOULD I PUT UP MY ARMOR
KEEP MY DISTANCE AND PLAY IT CALM AND COOL

BLAKE:
>SURE THIS GAL IS A BRIGHT ONE
>SURE SHE MIGHT BE THE RIGHT ONE
>WHY DO I FEEL LIKE I'M BACK IN GRAMMAR SCHOOL
>STILL I KNOW THAT
>
>YOU PLUS ME,

CAROL:
>I AGREE

BLAKE:
>MIGHT BE FUN,

CAROL:
>MIGHT BE MISERY

BLAKE:
>WHO CAN TELL, WELL, I'M FEELING RESOLUTE
>AND DETERMINED
>SHOULD I ASK HER OUT

CAROL:
>SHOULD WE MAKE A DATE

CAROL & BLAKE:
>LET'S NOT HESITATE— NO SIR
>THOUGH WE REALLY DON'T HAVE A CLUE
>BUT YOU'VE GOTTA JUST CHANCE IT WHEN YOU
>MEET CUTE

>>*Lights blackout on them. Lights up on Carol's office. ODETTE is there.*

ODETTE: "Static electricity?"

CAROL: Oh. It was more.

ODETTE: So, what happened? Seemed like that relationship had potential. And the Forresters. You were an intern? I wonder why your mind chose that night.

CAROL: We just had an intern start here today. And it reminded me of when I—

>*She stops.*

And Blake's outside, waiting to see me.

ODETTE: Feeling alone? Christmas? It's natural.

CAROL: I don't have time to be lonely.

ODETTE: What do you have time for? You've built this empire. You're successful—

CAROL: But this could collapse in a minute.

ODETTE: What happens with you and Blake? Let's try and go forward a bit...

Music in.

Concentrate on my voice... float... Go back...

SONG #7A: CLOSE YOUR EYES (CONTINUED)

(Singing)
CLOSE YOUR EYES THERE'S NOTHING YOU SHOULD FEAR
CLOSE YOUR EYES
AND SEE THINGS CRYSTAL CLEAR
AND IN FOCUS
WHAT YOU MAY HAVE LOST AND
WHAT IT MAY HAVE COST AND
BACK TO THE CHOICES THAT YOU'VE MADE SO FAR
AND MAYBE BACK TO THE THINGS
THAT MADE YOU WHO YOU ARE

Lights crossfade to another area. Carol's apartment. Christmas Eve. There are packed movie boxes everywhere. CAROL, wearing a work-shirt is labeling boxes. She lets BLAKE in.

BLAKE: I'm here. I'm starving. Let's eat. You're already packed? I don't have the U-Haul till next week.

CAROL: I'm actually leaving tomorrow.

BLAKE: You're going to Philly early?

CAROL: I'm not going to Philly.

BLAKE: What?

CAROL: There's nothing for me in Philly.

BLAKE: There's me.

(Beat)

Aren't you the girl who's going to move in with me?

CAROL: I thought so.

BLAKE: What's happened?

CAROL: I got a job offer in New York.

BLAKE: I didn't even know you were applying? Am I that out of it?

CAROL: It was a referral.

BLAKE: Carol... How can you...? We never even discussed—

He stops.

Is there room for negotiation here? It's Christmas Eve. We have reservations at Tony's that—

CAROL: I know. The timing sucks.

BLAKE: You'd really do this?

CAROL: I thought a lot about it the last two days.

BLAKE: But you said nothing. Where was I?

CAROL: At the hospital, saving lives, being a hero.

>   *(Beat)*

I know I'm a lousy person. Maybe it's better this way. I wouldn't be happy there. You'll be gone 24/7 during your residency.

BLAKE: We could try it. Don't we, at least, deserve a chance?

CAROL: Blake, I'm a planner, a dreamer, a schemer. This job is perfect for me. The timing—

BLAKE: Is there someone else?

CAROL: My career. I won't be happy as a doctor's wife, believe me.

BLAKE: You're not joking?

CAROL: No.

BLAKE: No discussion?

CAROL: No. I've made up my mind.

BLAKE: So, no happy ending for us?

CAROL: Blake...

>   *Music comes in.*

BLAKE: So...

CAROL: So...

SONG #8: SEPARATE WAYS

BLAKE:
>   WHAT A FINE WAY THIS TURNED OUT
>   WHAT A FINE PLACE WE'RE IN
>   TWO WHO CANNOT FIND THEIR WAY
>   SO WHO KNOWS WHAT MIGHT HAVE BEEN
>   GUESS WE'LL HAVE TO GRIEVE
>   ON THIS CHRISTMAS EVE
>   AND CHRISTMAS WON'T BE VERY MERRY
>   WHEN WE'RE BEING QUITE CONTRARY
>
>   WE'LL GO OUR SEPARATE WAYS
>   YOU TO YOUR LIFE
>   ME TO MINE

BLAKE (CONT'D):
> I GUESS WE NEVER GET OUR CHANCE
> TO BE TOGETHER
> CLOSE THE CHAPTER OF THIS BOOK AND JUST MOVE ON
>
> AND ALL THOSE NIGHTS AND DAYS
> ALL THE LAUGHTER
> ALL THE LOVE
> I GUESS THAT SIMPLY DISAPPEARS
> ALL IN THE PAST NOW
> AND THE DREAMS WE MIGHT HAVE SHARED,
> THOSE DREAMS ARE GONE
>
> TWO PEOPLE ON A DIFFERENT PATH
> SOMETIMES THOSE PATHS DON'T MEET
> TWO PEOPLE WHO, DESPITE THEIR FEELINGS
> CANNOT BE COMPLETE
> DESPITE THE SHARING AND THE CARING
> THE END IS BITTERSWEET
> GOALS TO MAKE
> HEARTS TO BREAK
>
> AND THOUGH THE HEARTBREAK STAYS
> WE SURVIVE AND WE MAKE DO
> I GUESS WE NEVER GET TO SEE
> THAT HAPPY ENDING
> THAT'S THE WAY THIS STORY PLAYS
> AS WE GO OUR SEPARATE WAYS— AS WE GO OUR SEPARATE WAYS
> AND SAY GOODBYE.

BLAKE exits. CAROL is alone in the apartment. Lights crossfade back to Carol's office.

ODETTE: Do you still feel that spark, that shock?

CAROL: Who has time?

ODETTE: Well, think about this. That's the point of what we're doing.

CAROL: Okay.

ODETTE: Now that you see the point, I think you know what you have to do.

CAROL: I have to open that package, don't I?

ODETTE: Right. The present is a gift. I'll leave you now.

CAROL: Thanks for making the office call. Blythe will take care of your bill.

ODETTE: Oh. I already received payment for today's visit... months ago. Doubled.

She exits as BLYTHE, FIONA, and AVALON enter with a box of paperwork.

BLYTHE: It's six o'clock.

CAROL: So.

BLYTHE: It's Christmas Eve.

CAROL: There's so much to do. It's not going to kill anyone to stay an extra fifteen minutes.

BLYTHE: It'll be fifteen, then another fifteen and then the "Oh! One more fifteen?" I sent everyone home.

CAROL: You're fired.

BLYTHE: Again?

CAROL: Couldn't we have cherry-picked a few people and hung on till seven?

BLYTHE: Clean break. Six PM. We're going and so should you.

CAROL: Fiona, can you just help me with a few things?

FIONA: I'd love to, but I have to get ready for my party. Remember, you're invited.

AVALON: I can stay.

BLYTHE *(to Avalon)*: No. Fiona will show you how to lock up. Go.

She ushers FIONA and AVALON out.

AVALON: Merry Christmas.

FIONA: Hope to see you later.

FIONA and AVALON exit. BLYTHE gives CAROL the box of paperwork.

BLYTHE: I feel like I'm giving you the Royal Box of paperwork, like the Queen has to go through every day.

CAROL: What are you in such a hurry about?

BLYTHE: I have a family waiting.

CAROL: It's fine. Go.

BLYTHE starts to exit.

BLYTHE: Merry Christmas, Carol. Sorry, I had to say it.

As she exits.

Hurry home.

BLAKE *(as he enters)*: Remember me?

CAROL: Crazy day.

BLAKE: I wrote an entire article that I'd been putting off out there and—

CAROL: What is this short proposal?

BLAKE: Oh? Is this my window?

CAROL: Quick. It's closing.

BLAKE: I'm going to Paris. Come with me.

CAROL: I go to Paris every year for the fashion shows.

BLAKE: Yes. You go, but you don't "land." You touch down on the runway, you limo to the hotel, you limo to the runways, but all you ever see of Paris is the hotel, the clothes and the blurry street scenes behind the tinted glass of your hired car.

CAROL: I'm kinda Paris'd out.

BLAKE: I want to show you a new-to-you-real-Paris.

He waits for her to interrupt, but she doesn't.

I have access to a private plane and a flat, not a hotel.

CAROL: I need room service and a 24/7 concierge squadron.

BLAKE: To do what? Relax?

(Beat)

You can tell me anything you want and I'll listen. I won't judge, just listen. You can get away from all this and get a new perspective.

CAROL: What's in it for you?

BLAKE: You. Alone. We can depart when you want and we can return when you want.

CAROL *(beat)*: We've been here before, haven't we? How long is this extravagant offer open?

BLAKE: Till midnight. You'll call me?

CAROL: I will.

BLAKE kisses her on the cheek.

BLAKE: Happy Christmas.

CAROL: Yeah, yeah, yeah.

BLAKE exits.

May as well finish this work at home. Christmas, who needs it?

CAROL starts to pick up her stuff the music begins.

SONG #8A: ALL I WANT FOR CHRISTMAS (REPRISE)

(Slowly)
ALL I WANT FOR CHRISTMAS
IS FOR ALL OF THIS TO STOP

A CAROL CHRISTMAS

CAROL (CONT'D):
CAN'T WE HAVE A CHRISTMAS
WHERE WE WORK UNTIL WE DROP

As CAROL gathers her stuff the tempo accelerates.

ALL OF THESE DISTRACTIONS
THEY'RE ALL DRIVING ME INSANE
AND THAT'S NOT A LONG DRIVE
AND I DON'T MEAN TO COMPLAIN
CHRISTMAS SEASON YOU CAN KEEP IT
HOW I FEEL, WELL, BETTER BLEEP IT
I'LL BE HAPPY WHEN IT'S IN THE PAST
WITH NO MORE YULETIDES AND SLEIGHRIDES AND JINGLE BELLS
AND SANTA CLAUS AND CHRISTMAS
IS DONE AT LAST!

Lights fade out on office as CAROLERS enter and the scene shifts to Carol's Loft/Home.

SONG #9: CHRISTMAS TIME IS HERE AGAIN (TRANSITION 1)

(Singing)
CHRISTMAS EVE IS ALMOST HERE
AND PEOPLE EVERYWHERE
GATHER WITH THE ONES THEY LOVE
TO CELEBRATE AND SHARE
CHRISTMAS TIDINGS, CHRISTMAS JOY
AND ALL IS CALM AND BRIGHT
CHRISTMAS WISHES LARGE AND SMALL
WONDER WHAT GIFTS AND SURPRISES ARE
COMING TO YOU TONIGHT
COMING TO YOU TONIGHT
COMING TO YOU TONIGHT

Their voices echo off as lights go full on Carol's loft.

Lights fade, as do their voices.

SCENE 4
CAROL'S LOFT

CAROL is set up to work all night. She's got a beverage, her laptop, her iPhone and the box of work from Blythe. The doorbell-tied-into-her-phone rings. She answers her phone on speaker.

CAROL *(into phone)*: This better be good because you're interrupting my workflow.

KARINA *(on speaker)*: Is me! Karina! Time for session!

CAROL *(into phone and looking at screen)*: What are you talking about?

KARINA *(on speaker)*: We have appointment now yes?

CAROL *(into phone)*: Now, no!

KARINA *(on speaker)*: Yes. Set up many month ago.

CAROL *(to herself)*: Joelle! I'd kill her but she's already most sincerely dead.

KARINA *(on speaker)*: What you say?

CAROL *(into phone)*: I'm buzzing you in.

KARINA *(on speaker, after buzzer sound)*: I come.

CAROL *(calling offstage)*: In here.

> *(To self)*

I'm turning off this phone: "Do Not Disturb."

KARINA *(offstage)*: I already brew tea. Starbuck thermos keep hot.

> *As she enters and begins to set up her paraphernalia:*

Let me unpack. Is freeze outside. Pittsburgh cold like Leningrad but uglier.

CAROL: I thought our appointment was in January, start the new year off with clarity, clear vision.

KARINA: Yes, after Russian Christmas. Was good for me. I get the text message from your office say, "December 24th. Must meet. Urgent."

CAROL: Joelle.

KARINA: Ah. Old dead partner? She send text from mausoleum?

CAROL: No. She had it sent.

KARINA: We begin now.

> *She lights candle and waves smoke to CAROL.*

You ready for the Owaska tea?

CAROL: As psychoactive herbal brews go, does it still taste like old socks?

KARINA: Yes, but good old socks. Make you hear better! Make you see better! Make you mind light up!

CAROL: You sure about this? Last time I was so sick.

A CAROL CHRISTMAS

KARINA: Last time, first time. Now, body stronger. Just relax. Calm the down. No talk. Can you no talk?

CAROL: Impossible. If I'm awake, I'm yappin'.

KARINA: What is yappin'?

CAROL: Constant talking, like a little dog barking.

KARINA: Yes, you the yappin'. Deep breathe.

CAROL: Okay.

KARINA: Owaska tea help you see what is what. Here. You drink now.

SONG #10: OWASKA TEA

KARINA:
>OWASKA TEA— VERY POWERFUL

CAROL: I know, it didn't do much for me.

KARINA:
>OWASKA TEA— VERY POTENT, VERY STRONG
>OWASKA TEA CAN HELP YOU HAVE
>CLARI-<u>TY</u>
>CHARI-<u>TY</u>
>SINCERI-<u>TY</u>
>POPULARI-<u>TY</u>
>>*(Speaking)*

You could use some of that, let me tell you.

CAROL *(she takes a sip— after a moment)*: Whoa, I feel strange— not like the last time.

KARINA *(smiling)*: I make the stronger dose. Drink, drink...
>*(Singing)*
>DRINK YOUR TEA AND SEE THE WORLD THAT'S AROUND YOU
>RIGHT IN FRONT OF YOU
>DON'T SEE WHAT YOU WANT TO SEE— SEE WHAT'S REALLY THERE
>WHAT YOU SEE— REALITY— MIGHT ASTOUND YOU
>IF YOU TAKE THE TIME TO OBSERVE
>WHAT YOU SEE MIGHT UNNERVE YOU
>THEN AGAIN IT MIGHT SERVE YOU WELL IF YOU LET IT
>IF YOU "GET" IT
>
>DRINK RIGHT UP, THAT CUP PUTS MAGIC INSIDE YOU
>IT'S A SPECIAL BREW
>I CAN'T TELL YOU WHAT IT IS— BUT IT'S POWERFUL

KARINA (CONT'D):
>SHAMANS SAY YOU'LL FIND YOUR WAY— LET ME GUIDE YOU
>AND SO LET THE TEA TAKE EFFECT
>THEN WE'LL START TO INSPECT THINGS
>MAYBE START TO CORRECT THINGS— GIVE IN, DON'T FIGHT IT
>JUST IGNITE IT

CAROL: Are you sure you're a real shaman?

KARINA *(speaks)*: What is real?

>*(Singing)*
>IT'S TRUE A RUSSIAN SHAMAN
>ISN'T REALLY COMMON
>LIKE A RUSSIAN RAPPIN'
>IT'S VERY RARE BUT IT CAN HAPPEN

>*Music changes to rap beat.*

>*(Raps)*
>ETOT CHAY RASSHIRIT VASH RAZUM
>I TY NAYDESH' SVOYU PRAVDU PRYAMO PERED SOBOY
>I TO, CHTO VY DELAYETE S ISTINOY— ETO TO, CHTO VY DELAYETE
>TAK SDELAYTE ETO, SDELAYTE ETO, SDELAYTE ETO

>*(Singing)*
>SEE WHAT I'M TELLING YOU
>I'M NOT JUST SELLING YOU

>*(Speaking)*

As sure as my name is Karina Anastasia Kateryna Yulia Yelyzaveta Oleksandra Markeyevich, I tell you true.

>*(Singing)*
>NOW IT'S TIME SO CLIMB ABOARD FOR YOUR TRIP NOW
>ANY MINUTE NOW
>BUCKLE UP, YOU MIGHT BE IN FOR A BUMPY NIGHT
>HERE WE GO, ON WITH THE SHOW, ONE MORE SIP NOW
>AND YOU'LL START TO SEE WHAT YOU SEE
>WHAT YOU SEE MIGHT JUST FREE YOU
>MAYBE YOU CAN JUST BE YOU— YOU THAT IS LURKING
>TEA IS WORKING
>SO, CLOSE YOUR EYES
>VISUALIZE
>AND SURPRISE
>HERE WE GO!

CAROL: Oh! My head! It's like I studied for the test and all the answers are banging on the door waiting to come out.

KARINA: Good. Good. Now. Focus. What answer knock loudest?

CAROL: Oh, my God. Who is this? What am I seeing? What trainwreck is this?

CAROL *(as Carol)*: Go sing on the fourth floor... deadlines are deadlines... let's do it when I said "artichoke green" I meant the inside tender parts of the leaves, not the dried, old, dark, dirty stem color. Use your head—read my mind! Who are these people? ...Make them go away... Did I butt-dial you? Intern whose name I can't remember... some days I have to go to DEFCON 1... Everyone out... I rest my case. Yeah, whatever, out, out, out, OUT!

KARINA: That you. Today. You see you?

CAROL: Yes. It's like an embarrassing acid trip flashback.

KARINA: You drink more, see more. What worry you most?

CAROL: Work—

KARINA: Where your family tonight?

CAROL: I don't really have much family... to speak of. My niece, Fiona.

KARINA: What you see with Fiona?

CAROL: She's too good to be true. She's having a party tonight. She invites me every year. I never go.

KARINA: Why?

CAROL: I never have. It's too hard to start now.

KARINA: What you think she does this minute?

> *Lights fade down somewhat on CAROL and KARINA. Lights fade up on scrim. We see FIONA and two girlfriends cutting up vegetables and making dip for her party.*

PATTY: So, you invited your aunt Carol again, right?

JOSIE: She won't come. She never does.

FIONA: She might.

JOSIE: She's too busy counting her money.

FIONA: A lot of things are different this year.

PATTY: Like what?

JOSIE: Did you get a promotion?

FIONA: No. But I got a boyfriend.

PATTY: Oh, right.

JOSIE: Are we going to meet him tonight?

FIONA: Yes. Right now.

> *(Calling)*

Howie?

HOWIE *(as he enters wearing a matching apron)*: Hi, everyone.

FIONA: Isn't he adorable. He's my own Jewish stock-broker.

HOWIE: Hello, ladies.

FIONA: This is Patty and Josie.

HOWIE *(to Fiona)*: Did you tell them that I'm kidnapping you tomorrow and you're meeting my family?

FIONA: You just did.

>*Music in.*

It's going to be a whole different kind of holiday this year.

PATTY: Why?

SONG #11: THIS CHRISTMAS

FIONA:
>THIS CHRISTMAS
>I'LL BE CELEBRATING HANUKKAH
>WITH THIS JEWISH MAN I'M DATING
>WON'T BE STANDING UNDERNEATH THE MISTLETOE THIS YEAR
>'CAUSE I'LL BE HERE WITH YOU.
>
>THIS CHRISTMAS
>I'LL BE LIGHTING A MENORAH
>SINGING, "DREIDL, DREIDL, DREIDL"
>SANTA WON'T BE COMING TO YOUR HOUSE
>BUT I'LL BE THERE, AN HONORARY JEW.
>
>ON THE 8TH DAY OF HANUKKAH, MY TRUE LOVE GAVE TO ME
>SOME LATKES AND A LOT OF CHOCOLATE GELT
>NO HE WON'T BE SAYING, "MERRY CHRISTMAS, DARLING,"
>BUT WHEN HE SAYS, "SHALOM," I SIMPLY MELT.
>
>THIS CHRISTMAS
>WON'T BE ROASTING ANY CHESTNUTS
>WON'T BE MIXING MEAT AND DAIRY
>STILL WE'LL HAVE A MERRY HOLIDAY
>FOR ME, FOR YOU, A GOY, A JEW
>A HAPPY HANUKKAH FOR TWO
>THIS CHRISTMAS, HANUKKAH IS WHAT WE'LL DO.
>THIS CHRISTMAS, HANUKKAH IS WHAT WE'LL DO. OY!

>*EVERYONE laughs and parties as the lights fade back to Carol's Loft.*

A CAROL CHRISTMAS

CAROL: She's got a boyfriend, and he's got a goy friend. That's why she's been so preoccupied.

KARINA: You go her party.

CAROL: I hate parties.

KARINA: Something else trouble you. Karina know.

CAROL *(after sipping tea)*: Blythe.

KARINA: What you see? Describe all.

CAROL: She has a daughter. Supposedly there is something wrong with her heart. But she seemed fine on bring-your-daughter-to-work-day.

KARINA: I wonder what going on in that house now. Tell me what tea makes you see.

The lights dim to half on CAROL and KARINA and fade up on a table at Blythe's house. FELIX, her husband, is reading to TRINA who is laughing. BLYTHE enters from the kitchen wearing an apron. She's re-arranging cookie sheets, and cookie mixture. Trina is working with the cookie dough.

TRINA: One down. Seven hundred and ninety-nine more to go.

BLYTHE *(to Trina)*: How was your day today?

TRINA: Fun. How about you?

BLYTHE: Busy. Crazy. Frustrating.

TRINA: Why, Mommy?

BLYTHE: I just couldn't go fast enough. I knew there were 600 things to do and I was only on 35.

TRINA: I wish I could come and help you like before.

BLYTHE: You will. Soon.

TRINA: Do you think that Santa will bring me a new heart?

FELIX: You're going to get better with your own heart.

TRINA: What about the transplant you told me about?

FELIX: That's risky.

TRINA: But, there can be success, right?

FELIX: Yes. Most times.

TRINA: I've made four. Is that enough? I'm tired all of a sudden.

BLYTHE: Do you want to help me bake them? And you can smell that warm peppermint smell and watch the twists merge?

TRINA: I can smell from over here.

FELIX *(settling Trina into a chair with a blanket and whispering)*: I'm going to go wrap those gifts for Mom that we picked out.

TRINA *(whispered)*: I was going to help you.

FELIX *(whispered)*: You already helped with the hardest part.

He exits.

BLYTHE *(crossing to Trina)*: Okay. First batch is in the oven. How you doin'?

TRINA: I'm trying hard not to be mopey.

BLYTHE: Good. It's Christmas Eve, what—?

TRINA: Will I ever get better?

BLYTHE: Of course you will.

TRINA: I want to go caroling with my friends, I want to help Daddy wrap presents, I want to help you bake cookies. I feel like I'm on slo-mo.

BLYTHE: Trina...

SONG #12: LITTLE MIRACLES

(Singing)
YOU MAY HAVE A WEAK HEART
BUT IT'S A UNIQUE HEART
A HEART AS BIG AS ALL OUTDOORS
THAT'S THAT HEART OF YOURS
YOU'VE GOT TO KEEP YOUR SPIRITS HIGH
AND BID YOUR FEARS A SWIFT GOODBYE
KEEP YOUR EYE ON ALL YOUR HOPES
AND DON'T GIVE IN TO THE MOPES
LISTEN CAREFULLY

THE WORLD IS FILLED WITH LITTLE MIRACLES
AND THOUGH SOMETIMES THEY MIGHT PASS YOU BY
THERE COMES A DAY WHEN ONE LITTLE MIRACLE
STOPS— AND LOOKS YOU IN THE EYE
AND SAYS "TODAY'S YOUR LITTLE MIRACLE
THE ONE THAT YOU'VE BEEN WAITING FOR"
AND THEN YOU GET YOUR LITTLE MIRACLE
AND YOU DON'T HAVE TO WAIT ANYMORE

AND EVERY DAY BRINGS LITTLE MIRACLES
YOU CAN'T PREDICT WHEN THEY MIGHT APPEAR
DON'T GIVE UP HOPE FOR YOUR LITTLE MIRACLE
WAIT— COULD BE IT'S ALMOST HERE
AND SOMEDAY SOON THAT LITTLE MIRACLE
THE ONE THAT'S SLIGHTLY OVERDUE

A CAROL CHRISTMAS

BLYTHE (CONT'D):
IT ONLY TAKES THAT LITTLE MIRACLE
FOR ALL YOUR HOPES AND DREAMS TO COME TRUE.

WHEN YOU LEAST EXPECT IT
THAT'S WHEN IT COMES
YES, WHEN YOU LEAST EXPECT IT
THERE IT IS WITH BELLS AND DRUMS
SING ALONG WITH ME

BLYTHE & TRINA:
SO DON'T GIVE UP ON LITTLE MIRACLES
IF YOU GIVE UP THEY MAY GO ASTRAY
IF YOU BELIEVE IN LITTLE MIRACLES
THEY— COULD BE HERE ANY DAY
AND THEN YOU'LL HAVE YOUR LITTLE MIRACLE
THE DAY IT SHOWS UP AT YOUR DOOR
THE DAY YOU GET YOUR LITTLE MIRACLE
YES, THAT'S THE DAY THAT I'M WAITING FOR
YES, THAT'S THE MIRACULOUS DAY I'M WAITING FOR.

They hug as the lights crossfade back to CAROL and KARINA.

KARINA: So much think about.

She packs up her belongings.

CAROL: Yes.

KARINA: And no sick?

CAROL: No sick.

KARINA: You see? Owaska tea and Carol get along good now. But you never take alone. You need Karina here, yes?

CAROL: Yes. How much do I owe you?

KARINA: Oh. Pay already come. Double, yes. You dream good tonight. Owaska tea pump up the dream big time. Bye, bye.

She exits.

CAROL breathes a sigh of relief. She opens the box of homework on her desk and takes off her shoes. The Doorbell rings. CAROL stares at her phone.

CAROL: Now what?

(To phone)

I turned you off. Damn you!

She answers the door on her phone with the push of a button.

CAROL (CONT'D) *(into phone)*: Who is it? I can't see you.

MABEL *(on speaker)*: It's Mabel! We have an appointment, honey.

CAROL *(to herself)*: It never ends.

> *(Into phone)*

Okay. I'm buzzing you in.

> *She presses a button on her phone.*

MABEL *(offstage)*: I do not work on holidays. But I made an exception because your office was so insistent. And I can still squeeze in a Mass tonight.

> *(As she enters)*

Did you forget we had this appointment?

CAROL: I didn't forget. It was a gift from my late partner.

MABEL: Oh. Nasty vibes. You want me to skeedattle? I'm outta here, but I'm keepin' the money.

CAROL: You're here. Let's do this.

MABEL: The cards steered you right the first time, didn't they?

CAROL: Yes. They did. And I'm just going with the flow because this has to be the craziest day of the year.

MABEL: Set up here?

CAROL: Yes.

> *MABEL clears away some boxes from Carol's table and starts to set out her ceremonial cloth, candles and Tarot cards. She shuffles.*

Come on, already. Can't we just cut to the cards.

MABEL: Honey, I got to do my preparations. Let me get the cards warmed up and see what they have to say.

> *Music in as MABEL does her ceremonial, artful, delicate, push-around-the-table-shuffle of the Tarot cards.*

SONG #13: TAROT CARDS

> *(Singing)*
> TAROT CARDS
> THEY SHOW YOU THE FUTURE
> GOTTA KNOW
> THAT THEY RARELY LIE
> HERE THEY COME
> I'M TURNIN' 'EM OVER
> SCADEE-WABADA-DEEDOO
> THEY'RE COMIN' YOUR WAY

MABEL (CONT'D):
>TAROT CARDS
>AND I'M GONNA READ 'EM
>UP TO YOU
>IF YOU'RE GONNA HEAR
>IT'S THE GOOD
>THE BAD AND THE UGLY
>SCOOBA-OOBADA-BEEDOO
>WHAT CARDS DO YOU PLAY
>
>TAROT CARDS
>IT'S TIME TO GET READY
>GIRD YOUR LOINS
>'CAUSE WE'RE GONNA START
>UP TO FATE
>THE CARDS THAT ARE DEALT HERE
>SCOBEE-BLABIDI-DEEROO
>THERE'S NO MORE DELAY
>
>WILL YOU GET THE FOOL OR THE MOON OR THE SUN
>OR THE MAGICIAN OR MAYBE THE EMPRESS
>WILL YOU GET THE LOVERS, THE HERMIT OR STRENGTH,
>THE HANGED MAN, THE DEVIL, OR DEATH
>CARDS ARE HUMMIN' CARDS ARE COMIN'
>SO, LADY, JUST TAKE A DEEP BREATH
>
>TAROT CARDS
>LET'S SEE WHAT THEY SAY NOW
>SETTLE BACK
>YOU KNOW THE ROUTINE
>HERE WE GO
>BE CALM, COOL, AND STEADY
>SKEEDEE-DIDDLEDEE-DEE DUM
>THEY'RE COMING
>SQUEEDA-DOODLEE-ABOP-SHOOBOP
>YOUR WAY.

MABEL: There are tropical storm clouds growing dark in your head, honey.
CAROL: I'm fine.
MABEL: You would be very wrong about that.
CAROL: Am I in danger?

MABEL: Let's see what the cards say. Touch the deck.

CAROL: I'm nervous.

MABEL: Good. The cards deserve respect.

> *MABEL shuffles the cards in a loose shuffle, she guides CAROL to turn over a card and Mabel stands up excitedly.*

First card you turned up is a rare one: The High Priestess.

CAROL: The High Priestess? What does she signify?

MABEL: She is keeper of the answers hiding behind the veil of consciousness, honey. And she is a force to be reckoned with.

> *THE HIGH PRIESTESS enters.*

THE HIGH PRIESTESS: I am a force to be reckoned with!

SONG #13: I KNOW EVERYTHING, I SEE EVERYTHING

(Singing)
I KNOW EVERYTHING, I SEE EVERYTHING
I'VE GOT ALL THE ANSWERS
LONG BEFORE YOU'VE GOT THE QUESTIONS
I KNOW EVERYTHING, I SEE EVERYTHING
YOU NEED GOOD SOLUTIONS
OR YOU NEED SOME GOOD SUGGESTIONS
BUT WILL YOU BE LISTENING, WILL YOU BE LEARNING
OR WILL YOU BE RETURNING TO YOUR BAD OLD WAYS

CAROL: What "bad old ways"?

THE HIGH PRIESTESS:
I KNOW EVERYTHING, I SEE EVERYTHING
WHEN YOU'RE THE HIGH PRIESTESS
THERE IS NOT MUCH THAT YOU'RE MISSIN'
I KNOW EVERYTHING, I SEE EVERYTHING
SO WHY DON'T YOU SHUT UP AND JUST TRY FOR ONCE TO LISTEN
AND CHANGE, THAT'S THE TICKET YOU SHOULD BE EARNING
OR WILL YOU BE RETURNING TO YOUR BAD OLD DAYS

CAROL: Confrontational much?

THE HIGH PRIESTESS:
I'M JUST A KNOW-IT-ALL
AND I SHOW IT ALL
OPEN YOUR EYES AND SEE WHAT'S WAITING
OPEN YOUR EYES AND I AM STATING

A CAROL CHRISTMAS

THE HIGH PRIESTESS (CONT'D):
I KNOW EVERYTHING, I SEE EVERYTHING
THAT INCLUDES THE FUTURE
AND THE LIFE THAT YOU'LL BE LIVING
I KNOW EVERYTHING, I SEE EVERYTHING
AND YOU KNOW THE FUTURE CAN BE REALLY UNFORGIVING
YOUR EYES WILL BE OPENED, EARS WILL BE BURNING
INSTEAD OF JUST RETURNING YOU CAN REAPPRAISE

SO, SEE WHAT I SEE AND LISTEN AND LEARN
THOUGH FOR YOU THAT'S GONNA BE HARD
YES, SEE WHAT I SEE AND LISTEN AND LEARN
AND WHEN YOU ARE THROUGH GO TURN ANOTHER CARD.

She exits.

MABEL: Typically, honey, Ms. Priestess shows her pretty little self when there are changes to be made that will impact someone's future. She thinks you're hidin' somthin'.

CAROL: I'm an open book. I don't hide—

MABEL: Negatory. She thinks you do. She is the very face of mystery, faith and knowledge which she gains through her quiet understanding of the entire universe.

CAROL: That was quiet understanding?

MABEL: She also is the symbol of female spiritual power; the female Pope, if you will. Heed her, honey. She is warning you that if a change is not made, there is double-jeopardy in your future. And I ain't talking about no game show.

CAROL: What kind of change?

MABEL: You'll know. Here. Do what she said. Turn another card now.

CAROL selects a card and turns it over.

Oh, my, my, my, my, my. Damn!

CAROL *(reading card)*: The Lovers.

MABEL: Do you know how many people pray to get this card? A ton, I'm tellin' you.

CAROL: Does this mean what I think it does?

MABEL: It could mean two halves of one mind: the soul and the physical. It could also mean that you are going to find love or you have found love.

CAROL: No. No. It can't be that.

MABEL: Let's see.

A QUARTET enters and sings.

SONG #14: THE LOVERS

MABEL (CONT'D):
LOVERS, THEY DANCE THROUGH THEIR LIVES
LOVERS LOVE LOVE WHEN IT BLOSSOMS AND THRIVES
AND LOVE GETS THROUGH TURMOIL
AND LOVE GETS THROUGH STRIFE
AND LOVERS LIVE THROUGH LIVES THEY SHARE
WHEN YOU PUT LOVE AWAY ON A SHELF
AND YOU CARE FOR NO ONE BUT YOURSELF
WHEN YOU STAY BY YOURSELF
DAY BY DAY BY YOURSELF
WHEN YOU'RE JUST LIVING LIFE LOCKED AWAY BY YOURSELF
WITH NO LOVER
YOU CAN'T WEATHER
STORMS TOGETHER
THAT'S FOR LOVERS.

> *Music changes to ethereal and delicate. Two DANCERS enter and do a pas de deux which ends with the lovers not together.*

WHEN YOU'RE LIVING A LIFE ON YOUR OWN
THEN YOU'RE LIVING A LIFE ALL ALONE
WHEN YOU CRY YOU'RE ALONE, WHEN YOU DIE YOU'RE ALONE
WHEN YOU ALWAYS LET LOVE PASS YOU BY YOU'RE ALONE
NOT FOR LOVERS
THEY CAN WEATHER
STORMS TOGETHER
THAT'S THE LOVERS

> *The QUARTET and DANCERS exit.*

MABEL: Carol, now level with me, honey. Can you honestly sit there and tell your Mabel that there is no one, I mean <u>no one</u>, in your life that could possibly be your potential love-lift-us-up-where-we belong person?

CAROL: Well...

MABEL: Okay. Then, you need to go for it. Now or never time. Let's do another card because that one is talkin' loud and clear.

> *CAROL pushes the cards around and selects one from the bottom. MABEL jumps up and stands back from the table.*

No! No, you did not just pull that card. Am I seein' things? "Death?"

A CAROL CHRISTMAS 43

CAROL: That looks very scary. So, I'm going to fall in love which has eluded me my whole life and then die. It's kinda like "Love Story" only with jingle bells.

MABEL: Easy now. Yes. It can mean you or someone near you will die. Are there likely candidates? An elderly uncle in an iron lung?

CAROL: Not that I can think of right now.

MABEL: This could be bad. Do not mess with Mr. Death.

> *The DEATH-MATES enter in a solemn procession, they're all holding little Hamlet skulls.*

DEATH-MATES *(chanting):* Hic mortis est

Hic mortis est

Hic mortis est

> *The DEATH-MATES part to reveal MR. DEATH. He sings.*

SONG #15: SHUFFLE OFF THIS MORAL COIL

MR. DEATH:
IT'S NOT LOOKIN' TOO GOOD, MY FRIEND
KEEP IT UP YOU'LL MEET A BITTER END
IT'S RIGHT BACK INTO THE SOIL
WHEN YOU SHUFFLE OFF THIS MORTAL COIL
YOU'LL BE A GONER

FAME AND FORTUNE, THAT'S WHAT YOU TRUST
LOT OF GOOD THEY'LL DO WHEN YOU ARE DUST
YOU'LL STILL BE BURNIN' THE OIL
WHEN YOU SHUFFLE OFF THIS MORTAL COIL
A MOVER-ONNER

WHEN DEATH COMES YOU'LL BE ALONE
PERHAPS IT'S TIME THAT YOU ATONE
PERHAPS IT'S TIME TO REASSESS
AND NOT TRY TO SECOND-GUESS
WHEN THE DEATH CARD IS REVERSED
YOU'RE AVERSE TO CHANGE
BUT WHEN THE DEATH CARD IS UPRIGHT
THERE CAN BE NEW BEGINNINGS, BRAND NEW INNINGS,
BRAND NEW WINNINGS FOR YOU TO TAKE
SO, UPRIGHT OR REVERSED
OPEN TO CHANGE OR CURSED

MR. DEATH (CONT'D):
>THE CHOICE IS YOURS TO MAKE
>DANCE BREAK
>A FIVE-SIX-SEVEN-EIGHT

Soft shoe dance break, then:

>NOW I'M DONE HERE, YOU'VE HEARD MY SPIEL
>WHAT YOU DO FROM HERE ON IN'S YOUR DEAL
>FOR FATE'S NOT SOMETHING YOU FOIL
>WHEN YOU SHUFFLE OFF THIS MORTAL COIL!

The DEATH FIGURES fade away.

CAROL: Should I be scared?

MABEL: You can be if you want to. The Tarot has presented water color possibles for you, honey. If fear gets your engine running, then get on that rollercoaster.

CAROL: The Tarot cards have helped me in the past with hard decisions and I've done well, but—

MABEL *(collecting her Tarot cards)*: These cards are not your Mardi Gras street-side fortune tellers. They bring you focus. Let their message--their warnings— wash over ya. They're gonna mean more to you than anybody else. I gotta go. Hit that mass.

CAROL: Did my office already take care of your bill?

MABEL: You know they did, sweetheart... and double! Good luck now.

She exits.

CAROL: I am exhausted.

She sits down at table, takes out some paperwork, sips her drink and falls asleep.

SONG #16: NIGHTMARE

As CAROL sleeps we see her nightmare come to life— bits and pieces from her sessions with ODETTE, KARINA, and MABEL— a giant melange of Carol's snappish behavior, her choices, her unawareness of what's going on around her, all sung in great dissonance against music we've been hearing throughout the show, building to a huge cacophony of sound and image all closing in on Carol as she twists and turns uncomfortably on her couch until she finally bolts awake, at which point her nightmare, in sound and vision, disappears.

CAROL: Oh, my God. I didn't die. That's it. Enough. I have to change my life now. I've been a terrible person.

She picks up the phone.

A CAROL CHRISTMAS

CAROL (CONT'D) *(into phone):* Avalon? Get dressed. I'm sending a car for you.

She hangs up and speed dials another number.

Blake... I have a favor to ask. One of my employees— probably my most cherished employee, has a child that may need a heart transplant... When did Blythe send you Trina's chart? Oh, so you haven't had time to look at it yet? Can you evaluate and deploy your research skills and come up with a recommendation? Tonight? Yes, now. It would mean the world to me. Ok, bye.

She hangs up and speed dials another number.

Pearlman, Carol. Sorry to bother you after hours, but I've reconsidered. Meet me at Fiona's place and I'll take your advice on those charities. Yes, now... and bring the partnership papers.

She hangs up.

All right, Christmas. Here we come.

Lights fade on loft as CAROL crosses out.

Where are my beautiful carolers?

Lights up on the CAROLERS.

Follow me! We're going to Fiona's house!

CAROL and the CAROLERS lead us to Fiona's party. Carol, AVALON and other employees join them and they enter en masse.

SONG #16A: CHRISTMAS TIME IS HERE AGAIN (TRANSITION 2)

(Singing)
AS WE GO FROM DOOR TO DOOR
TO SPREAD THE CHRISTMAS CHEER
LET US BRING THE JOY AND LIGHT
TO ALL THOSE WE HOLD DEAR

They arrive at Fiona's.

FIONA: Carol! You came!

CAROL: Wouldn't miss it. Merry Christmas, Fiona.

She hugs Fiona.

FIONA: This is such a surprise.

CAROL: If you don't have enough food, it's understandable. I know I've stood you up for many years.

FIONA: No. I don't look at it that way. It's an "Open House" and you can drop by whenever you want... or never.

CAROL: "Stood up." Clear and simple. But I brought my attorneys and I wanted to drop by, say hi, and tell you that I've taken your suggestion and we are creating a Social Media Marketing Division and you'll be in charge. Our newest Vice President.

    (To Petit and Pearlman)

Boys, paperwork her.

FIONA: What?

CAROL: Now, who wants to go with me to Blythe's house?

FIONA: Isn't it too late? If Trina's asleep—

CAROL: What kid goes to bed early on Christmas Eve?

FIONA: But if she's not feeling well—

CAROL: Then we need to bring them buckets of cheer. Come on! You, too, Carolers!

SONG #16B: CHRISTMAS TIME IS HERE AGAIN (TRANSITION 3)

    (Singing)
CHRISTMAS MAGIC FILLS THE AIR
THE HERALD ANGELS SING
AS WE WANDER THROUGH THE NIGHT
WHAT FLIGHTS OF FANCY WILL GREET US NOW
AND WHAT WILL THIS EVENING BRING

    CAROLERS, CAROL and others take us to Blythe and Felix's House. TRINA is dressed in adorable Christmas pajamas. BLYTHE and FELIX are prepping things for tomorrow.

FELIX: Come on. Bedtime.

TRINA: Can't I stay up and watch a movie, like last year?

FELIX: I don't know. Blythe?

TRINA: It might make me sleepy!

FELIX: Okay.

    Doorbell rings.

TRINA: Who could that be?

BLYTHE: A neighbor, maybe, wanting to borrow some ingredient for Santa cookies?

FELIX: Be careful.

BLYTHE *(offstage)*: Who is it?

CAROL *(offstage)*: The last person you'd ever expect to see tonight.

BLYTHE *(offstage, opening door)*: Carol?

A CAROL CHRISTMAS

CAROL: Yes. I brought my entourage to festive up your eve.

CAROL, PETIT & PEARLMAN, FIONA, AVALON and OTHERS walk in.

Where's Trina?

TRINA: Here I am.

CAROL: I didn't recognize you from bring-your-daughter-to-work day. You look so much more grown up.

TRINA: It's me.

CAROL: Give me a hug, you little elf.

TRINA: Do I know you?

BLYTHE: You know Carol.

TRINA: I know a grouchy Carol.

EVERYONE laughs.

CAROL: I'm trying to empty the grouch pouch.

TRINA: How come?

CAROL: I guess I got bit by the Christmas spirit.

FIONA *(to Trina)*: So, where are these candy cane cookies I've heard so much about?

TRINA: Here! Here! We have tons.

CAROL: We came to cheer up your mom.

BLYTHE: I'm fine.

CAROL: You are not. Let me cheer you up, dammit!

(To Trina)

Sorry.

TRINA: It's okay. I know that word.

FELIX: Would anyone like anything to drink?

CAROL: Do you think we'd show up empty-handed? We brought noshy things and punch and eggnog and bubbly.

BLYTHE: This is so very unexpected.

AVALON: Here. Let me set up a buffet.

CAROL: This one, watch her.

AVALON *(to Trina)*: Hi. I'm the intern.

TRINA: Hi. I'm Trina.

AVALON: Where should I set up?

BLYTHE: Over here.

TRINA: Carol?

CAROL: Yes, Trina.

TRINA: Why did you name your company Lora Co?

CAROL: Lora, spelled L-O-R-A was my mother's name and I added the "Co" just to make it sound more highfalutin'.

TRINA: Do you know what "Lora Co" spelled backwards is?

CAROL (thinking): Um...

(Thinking)

My mind doesn't work backwards.

TRINA: O Carol! Your name!

FIONA: That's incredible.

CAROL: O-Carol! I love it!

TRINA: You're welcome. You want to see my room?

CAROL: I'd love to.

She winks at BLYTHE.

BLYTHE: Carol doesn't want—

CAROL: I do.

FELIX (to Avalon): Come on. Let's get this all set up.

Lights crossfade to Trina's bedroom. CAROL and TRINA enter.

CAROL: This is lovely; so creative.

TRINA: Yeah. I'm still digging Disney.

CAROL: It's very methodical with a lot of attention to detail.

TRINA: Can we have a child-to-woman talk, O-Carol?

CAROL: Sure, hon. What's on your mind?

TRINA: My mother.

CAROL: Okay.

TRINA: Do you think you could run Lora Co without her?

CAROL: I don't know. Why? Are you acting as her agent and negotiating with other companies?

TRINA (she laughs): Not yet.

CAROL: Your mother is invaluable to me.

TRINA: That's what I thought. Your old partner died, right?

CAROL: Yes.

TRINA: Don't you think it's time for a new partner?

CAROL: Maybe. Did you have someone in mind?

TRINA: I like you. You're funnier than I remember.

CAROL: It's a brand new me.

A CAROL CHRISTMAS

TRINA: Great. Because I think you should make my mom your partner. Fifty-fifty.

CAROL: Just "give" her half?

TRINA: At least. Just think about it. She's very helpful to you now, but as a partner, she'd have more time to help you with those big decisions.

CAROL *(beat)*: You're very persuasive.

TRINA: That's my job until I become an intern.

CAROL: I have a confession.

TRINA: Go.

CAROL: This is something I've been contemplating.

TRINA: And I sealed the deal?

CAROL: You have, Trina.

TRINA: When can you do it?

CAROL: What would you say if I told you that I actually brought two attorneys with me tonight and that I had already instructed them to draw up partnership papers and they have those papers with them tonight?

TRINA: What would I say? I'd say, "Yay!" Let's tell her?

Light crossfade to Living Area. CAROL and TRINA cross in. Trina rings a large jingle bell.

Mom, Carol Claus here has a ginormous gift for you. She's giving you half of Lora Co and making you her official partner.

BLYTHE: Are you kidding me?

CAROL: She took the words right out of my mouth.

FELIX: This is great!

BLYTHE: Is this for real? Why is Trina announcing it?

CAROL: She brokered the deal.

BLYTHE: Trina?

TRINA: Truth: she already had the papers made up way before she got here. She let me feel like I was talking her into it.

CAROL *(to Blythe)*: Partner?

BLYTHE *(to Carol)*: Partner!

They embrace.

TRINA: Photo Op!

FIONA *(takes photo with her phone)*: We'll post this immediately.

Doorbell sounds.

FELIX: Who could that be?

FELIX crosses to door.

TRINA *(to Carol)*: Did you invite the rest of the staff?

BLAKE *(offstage)*: I'm looking for Carol. I'm Blake.

FELIX *(offstage)*: She's here. I'm Felix.

BLAKE: Carol!

CAROL: Hey, everyone, this is Blake.

CAROL walks up to BLAKE and kisses him on the mouth.

There's mistletoe here somewhere, right?

TRINA: Down the street, three houses, but close enough.

BLAKE *(to Trina)*: Are you Trina?

TRINA *(to Carol)*: He's so sharp. He's a keeper.

BLAKE: I didn't know if you were maybe a sister. You certainly don't look as ill as your medical charts make you sound.

TRINA: I'm wearing Disney Weatherproof Princess Make-up.

CAROL: This is Blake. We spent... our college years together and he was a doctor, now he's in research.

BLAKE *(to Trina)*: Your mom sent me your chart.

TRINA: How bad is it? You don't have to soften the truth for me.

BLAKE: Well, getting a heart transplant at this point seems unlikely. But what I feel and several doctors agree with me, is that a transplant may not be the best course of action.

BLYTHE: Why not?

BLAKE: While Trina's sporadic symptoms are severe, they're not as dire as other potential recipients. And heart transplants are no picnic. And the first thing your body does is try to reject the new heart.

TRINA: My body wouldn't.

BLAKE: You think that, but that's the body's natural defense; especially with kids.

CAROL: What do you recommend?

BLAKE: There is a drug trial we can put Trina into. We might be able to make your heart stronger and that would be a safer treatment plan.

TRINA: I put only one thing on my Christmas List: new heart

BLAKE: What I'm proposing is more curved and creative and you'd get to keep your own heart.

CAROL: Blake is the top in his field and he and I are going to make sure you get the best treatment possible; the most cutting edge-but-safest thing to do. Blake is my gift to you.

FELIX: This is exactly what we've been—

A CAROL CHRISTMAS

BLYTHE: Trina, sweet, smart, irrepressible child of mine, you wanted Santa to find a heart for you. And he did. Carol's heart. It was lost and now it's found.

CAROL: Everyone: I want you all to have the best Christmas ever because you know how much work there is after... the New Year. And I'm giving you all next week off.

>*All EMPLOYEES stand with their mouths open.*

BLYTHE: What happened tonight?

CAROL: So much. Let's say it was an eye-opener. And thanks to old Joelle, I picked up a few things.

BLYTHE: Like what?

SONG #17: WHAT HAVE I LEARNED

(Singing)
WHAT HAVE I LEARNED
I'LL TELL YOU WHAT I'VE LEARNED
THE PAST AND THE PRESENT
THEY WEREN'T VERY PLEASANT
SO THE THING TO DO IS TO
RECTIFY THE PAST
RECTIFY THE PRESENT
SO THE FUTURE CAN BE PLEASANT
AND I'M
TURNING OVER A BRAND NEW LEAF
TURN THE CORNER AND YOU WILL FIND THERE'S A
BRAND NEW PERSON
AND I
MAKE A VOW FROM THIS MOMENT ON
I'M GONNA TAKE THE TIME TO START LIVING
APPRECIATE THE THINGS I HAVE, AND START GIVING
AND THAT'S WHAT I'VE LEARNED

WHAT HAVE I LEARNED
I'VE LEARNED THAT THINGS CAN CHANGE
YES, I'VE BEEN CONTRARY
SOMETIMES PRETTY SCARY
BUT I SAW THE LIGHT AND SO
HERE'S TO SOMETHING NEW
HERE'S TO SOMETHING DARING
LIKE CONSIDERATE AND CARING

BLYTHE (CONT'D):
AND I'M
ON THE ROAD TO A WHOLE NEW LIFE
FLIP THE PAGE AND YOU'RE GONNA FIND
THERE'S A WHOLE NEW STORY
AND NOW
DID YOU EVER THINK THAT YOU'D SEE
SOMEONE WHO'S FUN AND FREE AND LIGHTHEARTED
AND I AM HERE TO SAY I'M JUST GETTING STARTED
AND THAT'S WHAT I'VE LEARNED

WHAT A DAY AND NIGHT THIS HAS BEEN
BUT I GUESS IT HAPPENED FOR A REASON
AND I HAVE TO ADMIT IT'S TRUE
IT'S STARTING TO FEEL LIKE THE CHRISTMAS SEASON

WHAT HAVE I LEARNED
I'LL TELL YOU WHAT I'VE LEARNED
TO SAVOR EACH MINUTE
FIND THE JOY THAT'S IN IT
I'VE ALREADY FOUND THAT'S MORE
FUN THAN BEING TENSE
WHO NEEDS ALL THAT WORRY
ALWAYS BEING IN A HURRY
AND HEY
LOOK, I'M SMILING— WELL, THAT'S A FIRST
LOOK I'M SINGING A SONG, I'M LIKE A
CHRISTMAS CAROL
AND I
WANT TO CELEBRATE ALL MY FRIENDS
AND THOUGH I KNOW THE SENTIMENT'S SAPPY
WELL, DAMN IT WHO'D HAVE THOUGHT THAT I COULD BE HAPPY
HAPPY
AND THAT'S WHAT I'VE LEARNED!

BLAKE and CAROL hug.

TRINA: Are you two an item?

BLAKE *(to Carol)*: I don't know. Are we an item?

CAROL: What's an item?

BLAKE: What we were many years ago.

CAROL: All I know is I'm going to Paris tomorrow.

A CAROL CHRISTMAS

TRINA: Enoyreve su sselb doG!

BLAKE: What?

CAROL: Wait. My brain is working backwards: God Bless Us, Everyone!

SONG #18: FINALE – IT'S A CAROL CHRISTMAS

(Singing)
IT'S A CAROL CHRISTMAS
IT'S A TIME WHEN EVERYTHING TURNS OUT RIGHT
AND THE FUTURE'S BRIGHT ON THIS MAGIC NIGHT
THOUGH IT MAY SOUND TRITE, THAT'S THE WAY THAT WE FEEL
IT'S A CAROL CHRISTMAS
IT'S A TIME FOR CELEBRATING AND FUN
AND WE WILL HAVE FUN, AND IT'S JUST BEGUN
ALL THE JOY AND WON—
DER THAT'S COMING YOUR WAY
IT'S A CAROL CHRISTMAS (WONDER COMING YOUR WAY)
IT'S A CAROL CHRISTMAS (WONDER COMING YOUR WAY)
IT'S A CAROL CHRISTMAS (WONDER COMING YOUR WAY)
GOD BLESS US EVERYONE ON CHRISTMAS DAY!
(Speaking)
It's a Carol Christmas!

Curtain.

END OF PLAY

STAGE RIGHTS

ABOUT STAGE RIGHTS

Based in Los Angeles and founded in 2000, Stage Rights is one of the foremost independent theatrical publishers in the United States, providing stage performance rights for a wide range of plays and musicals to theater companies, schools, and other producing organizations across the country and internationally. As a licensing agent, Stage Rights is committed to providing each producer the tools they need for financial and artistic success. Stage Rights is dedicated to the future of live theatre, offering special programs that champion new theatrical works.

To view all of our current plays and musicals, visit:

www.stagerights.com

Made in the USA
Coppell, TX
10 November 2021